U.S.
TERRITORIES
AND
FREELY
ASSOCIATED
STATES

U.S. TERRITORIES

AND FREELY ASSOCIATED STATES

TERRY DUNNAHOO

FRANKLIN WATTS 1988
NEW YORK LONDON TORONTO SYDNEY
A VENTURE BOOK

The material mentioned in this book was
up-to-date at the time of publication.

Library of Congress Cataloging-in-Publication Data

Dunnahoo, Terry.
U.S. territories and freely associated states / Terry Dunnahoo.
p.   cm.—(Venture Book)
Bibliography: p.
Includes index.
Summary: Introduces the major territorial possessions and
commonwealths of the United States, all of which are islands.
Includes Puerto Rico, the Virgin Islands, the Marianas, Guam,
American Samoa, and others.
ISBN 0-531-10605-5
1. United States—Territories and possessions—Juvenile
literature.   2. United States—Insular possessions—Juvenile
literature.   [1. United States—Territories and possessions.
2. United States—Insular possessions.]   I. Title.   II. Title: US
territories and freely associated states.
F965.D86 1988
973'.09'719—dc19   88-16982   CIP   AC

For my niece Lorraine
with love

CONTENTS

U.S.
TERRITORIES
AND
FREELY
ASSOCIATED
STATES

ONE

INTRODUCTION

Before becoming the forty-ninth and fiftieth states, Alaska and Hawaii were U.S. territories. Although Alaska and Hawaii are no longer territories, the United States still has other territories in the Caribbean Sea and in the Pacific Ocean. Some of these territories are small and uninhabited islands, which will never become states, but others may eventually reach the position of statehood.

The terms on page 14 explain some of the words used in this book and by the U.S. government to describe the status of its territories.

The places described in this book have three things in common. They are all islands, and they are all dependent on the United States for financial help and for protection in case of war. Some, like Wake and Midway Islands, are defense installations ready to help with that protection.

THE WORLD

GREENLAND

ALASKA

CANADA

NORTH
AMERICA

UNITED STATES

ATLANTIC
OCEAN

PACIFIC
OCEAN

MIDWAY ISLANDS

NAVASSA ISLAND

PUERTO RICO

MEXICO

CARIBBEAN SEA

U.S. VIRGIN ISLANDS

HAWAII

JOHNSTON ATOLL

CENTRAL AMERICA

HOWLAND
ISLAND

KINGMAN REEF

PALMYRA ISLAND

BAKER ISLAND

JARVIS ISLAND

WESTERN SAMOA

AMERICAN SAMOA

SOUTH
AMERICA

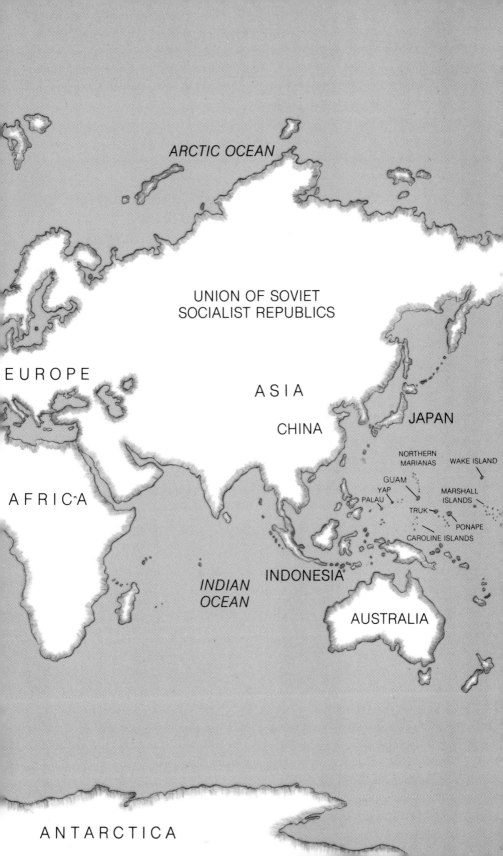

Territory—a place where the United States can make rules and regulations to protect its property.

Incorporated territory—a place where people use the Constitution of the United States.

Unincorporated territory—a place where the Constitution of the United States does not apply. An unincorporated territory may be organized or unorganized.

Organized territory—a place with a government much like the one of your own state.

Unorganized territory—a place that does not have an Organic Act, which provides the power to self-govern.

Possession—an unincorporated territory.

Commonwealth—a territory that has a high degree of local government under a constitution written and adopted by the people of that territory.

Trust Territory—a place administered by the United States under a United Nations charter.

The Commonwealth of Puerto Rico and the Virgin Islands are in the Caribbean Sea close to the United States. But American Samoa, Guam, the Commonwealth of the Northern Marianas, the Federated States of Micronesia, the Republic of the Marshall Islands, and the Republic of Palau are in the Pacific Ocean thousands of miles from mainland United States. Smaller territories such as Baker, Howland, Jarvis, Navassa, and Palmyra islands, Johnston Atoll, and Kingman Reef are uninhabited. All of the islands rely on the United States for the many reasons discussed in this book.

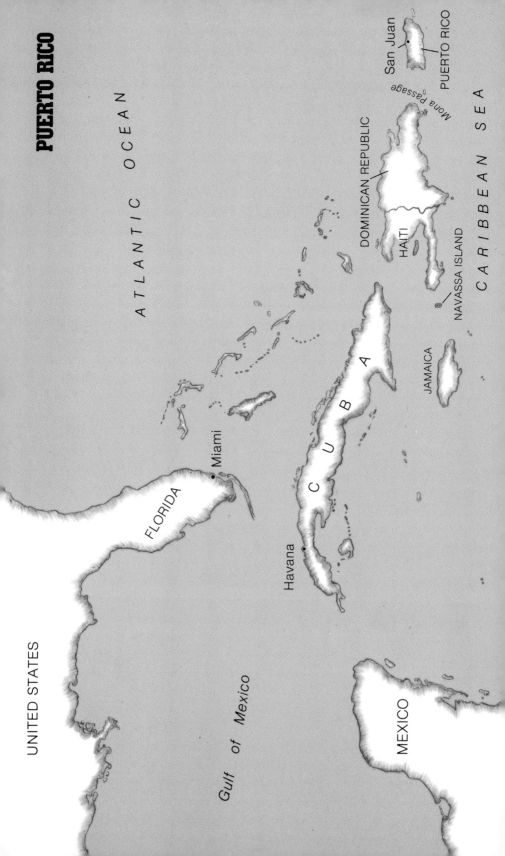

PUERTO RICO

UNITED STATES

ATLANTIC OCEAN

FLORIDA

Miami

Gulf of Mexico

Havana

C U B A

MEXICO

JAMAICA

DOMINICAN REPUBLIC

HAITI

NAVASSA ISLAND

CARIBBEAN SEA

Mona Passage

San Juan

PUERTO RICO

TWO

PUERTO RICO

Millions of years ago before people lived there, Puerto Rico was a peninsula that stretched out from Mexico and included what is now Cuba, Haiti, and the Dominican Republic. When the peninsula sank, only the peaks of the highest mountains remained above water. One of these peaks became the island of Puerto Rico.

Puerto Rico is bounded on the north and east by the Atlantic Ocean, on the south by the Caribbean Sea, and on the west by the Mona Passage. The island has 3,435 square miles (14,300 sq. km) and is twice the size of Delaware. Puerto Rico is about 100 miles long by 35 miles (160 km × 56 km) wide. It is 1,000 miles (1,600 km) southeast of Miami, Florida. There are about 3.4 million people living in Puerto Rico. The capital of Puerto Rico is San Juan.

*Hotels line San Juan's waterfront
of present-day Puerto Rico.*

DISCOVERY AND
COLONIZATION

The Arawak Indians from South America were probably the first settlers on Puerto Rico. They called the island *Borinquen*, which means "Land of the Brave." There were 30,000 Arawaks on the island when Christopher Columbus landed there on November 19, 1493, during his second trip to the New World. The Indians were fishermen and hunters who had built houses around village squares and set up an organized system of government. Columbus claimed the island for Spain and called it San Juan Bautista.

Columbus paid little attention to his new discovery, but Ponce de León, a member of his crew, thought it was the best of the islands Columbus had discovered. Ponce de León wanted to settle San Juan Bautista, but King Ferdinand of Spain made him governor of the Dominican Republic, instead. It took fifteen years before Ponce de León got his wish. On August 12, 1508, he landed on San Juan Bautista with fifty Spaniards to establish a settlement and search for gold.

The Arawaks helped the Spaniards build the city of Caparra on San Juan Bay where Spanish ships, coming from Mexico and loaded with gold, stopped on their way home to Spain. Ponce de León wanted to find gold on San Juan Bautista, but they only found small deposits. By the time de León learned this, he no longer had the friendship of the Arawak Indians.

De León forced the Arawaks to work as laborers on farms and in mines, and the peaceful Indians finally revolted. However, their primitive weapons were no match for the cannons of the Spaniards, and thousands of Indians were killed. During the years that followed, other

Arawaks died from diseases that were brought to their islands by the settlers, many committed suicide, and a small number escaped from the island.

In 1518, the Spaniards brought slaves from Africa to replace the Indian labor. During the next year the settlement at Caparra, which had been renamed Puerto Rico, was moved east to what is now San Juan. The name San Juan was given to the new city in 1521, and the island became known as Puerto Rico, which means "rich port." By that time, Ponce de León had lost his position as governor, but had discovered Florida and claimed it for Spain.

The governors who ruled after Ponce de León fortified San Juan against Spain's enemies. The French attacked the island several times during the mid-1500s, but there was no serious attack until 1595. That attack was led by Sir Francis Drake of England with a fleet of ships and an army of 4,500. Cannon fire from San Juan's fortifications drove the English off.

Three years later, the British attacked again. This time they captured San Juan and held it for five months, but abandoned it when an epidemic broke out. In 1625, the Dutch tried to invade the island but they were defeated.

After this attack the governmnent of Spain realized that, unless it turned San Juan into a fortress, the city and the island would eventually be taken by a foreign nation. In 1631, the Spanish began building a wall around the city. It took almost 150 years to complete. The British attacked again in 1787; despite their ships and an army of 7,000, they could not take the island. This was the last attack of any importance against Puerto Rico until American troops landed on the island in 1898 during the Spanish-American War.

A section of Morro Castle. This fortress was built by Ponce de León. Early in the 1500s, fortifications such as this one were constructed; they withstood numerous attacks, including one in 1898, hundreds of years later during the Spanish-American War.

THE SPANISH-
AMERICAN WAR

Between 1797 and 1898, the population of Puerto Rico grew. Rebels newly arrived in Puerto Rico from Spanish colonies in the Caribbean tried to convince the Puerto Ricans to revolt against Spain. Although minor outbreaks of rebellion among the residents occasionally broke out, most of the islanders remained loyal to Spain. In return, they asked for the right to help govern their island.

In 1809, the Puerto Ricans were permitted to choose their first delegate to the Spanish Parliament. With representation in Spain, they had the opportunity to work toward self-government, which would improve living conditions. But the Spanish Parliament was dissolved in 1814, and, with no one to represent the Puerto Ricans in Spain, the island's progress toward self-government stopped.

Through the work of Luis Muñoz Rivera, a poet and journalist, Puerto Rico was finally granted self-government by Spain. Then, in February 1898, only a few days after Puerto Rico's government took office, the American battleship *Maine* was blown up in Havana Harbor, Cuba. The Americans blamed the Spaniards for the disaster, and eight weeks later the United States declared war on Spain, beginning the Spanish-American War.

On July 18, 1898, a defeated Spain asked France to arrange an armistice with the United States. But before the armistice could take effect, American soldiers landed on Puerto Rico. They met little resistance and on October 18, 1898, the capital of San Juan surrendered to the Americans. Two months later, on December 10, 1898, the Treaty of Paris ended the Spanish-American War. That treaty gave Puerto Rico to the United States and ended Spain's 400-year rule of the island.

UNITED STATES TERRITORY

The United States placed Puerto Rico under military rule by the U.S. Navy. The island stayed under the Department of the Navy until 1900, when the United States passed the Foraker Act, also known as the Organic Act of 1900. Under the act, the first civil governor was appointed, and the people of Puerto Rico were allowed to elect a House of Delegates. Any legislation passed by the delegates, however, had to be approved by the governor. Therefore, although the House of Delegates gave Puerto Ricans a say in their government, their wishes could be denied by a governor appointed by the President of the United States. It was not until 1946 that the first Puerto Rican, Jesus Toribio Pinero, was appointed governor.

The Foraker Act made the islanders citizens of Puerto Rico, but not citizens of the United States. The act also gave Puerto Ricans the right to elect a representative to the U.S. Congress. This person would not have a vote in Congress, but could work to improve conditions on the island. Luis Muñoz Rivera, who was elected to that position in 1910, was partly responsible for the Jones Act, which was passed in 1917. The Jones Act did nothing to change the status of Puerto Rico, but it made the people citizens of the United States.

GROWTH AND INDUSTRY

Under Spanish rule, the people of Puerto Rico with the help of slaves grew cotton, ginger, sugar cane, coffee, and tobacco. When the slaves were freed in 1873, the farming continued, and agriculture was the main industry on the island when the United States acquired Puerto Rico.

Businesses from the United States built mills on the island to process sugar, tobacco, and rum. These products were taken to ships over a newly constructed railroad. The owners of the land and businesses became rich, while the average worker remained poor. The United States sent millions of dollars to Puerto Rico to help the poor inhabitants of the island. Although the money helped those who were the worst off, it failed to end the poverty.

The continuing poverty was caused partially by the population growth. As soon as Puerto Rico became a territory, the United States built roads, waterways, schools, and hospitals. The schools and hospitals created education and provided better health care for the islanders. The number of deaths was reduced, while the number of births rose. As the population of the island grew so did the number of poor people.

In 1942, the Puerto Rican Development Company was formed. The company became known as *Fomento*, which means "development" in Spanish. Fomento initially successfully built houses and small businesses, and then managed industries the government had started in order to create jobs. But the project had problems from the beginning. The island did not have many natural resources, World War II made it difficult to ship materials from the United States, and there was not enough electric power or trained workers to operate machinery. Five years later all but one factory was losing money, and poverty was still a major problem.

In 1949, the first governor elected by the citizens of Puerto Rico, instead of being appointed by the President of the United States, took office. This gave the local government more power, and with the help of Fomento, Operation Bootstrap was launched. This program promised

*Students of an industrial vocational
school in San Juan watch as their
instructor shows them how to operate
a machine. The school is affiliated
with Operation Bootstrap.*

businesses from the United States tax savings and low labor costs. Because this meant increased profits, American corporations started to build factories in Puerto Rico. Industries created on the island included food products, clothing, textiles, electronics, artificial kidneys, cameras, plastics, and tourism.

By 1955, manufacturing was bringing in more money than agriculture, and thousands of people moved from the countryside to the cities. So many people came to the cities that there were not enough jobs for everyone. Those who did find work bought houses, cars, and televisions. Shopping malls sprang up, highways were constructed, and hotels were built for the tourists who flocked to the island.

While many people were moving to the cities, one out of every five native Puerto Ricans was leaving the island for the United States. Having made the decision to leave the farms, the more ambitious decided to try a new life in the United States. Today, more Puerto Ricans live in New York City than in San Juan, the largest city in Puerto Rico.

If these people were living in Puerto Rico instead of the United States, the population of the island would be dangerously high. Despite a birth control program that began in 1937, thousands of babies are born each year. This overpopulation has kept half of the people on the island living in poverty, a problem the governments of Puerto Rico and the United States have not been able to correct.

GOVERNMENT

In 1947, the United States amended the Jones Act to allow the people of Puerto Rico to elect their own gov-

*Tourists at a Puerto Rican
hotel relaxing by the pool*

A street corner in a Puerto Rican neighborhood in New York City. Notice some shop signs are in English and others are in Spanish.

ernor. Luis Muñoz Marin, son of Luis Muñoz Rivera, won the election in 1948 and took office in 1949. He remained Puerto Rico's governor until 1964. In 1951, the U.S. Congress passed a law allowing Puerto Rico to write its own constitution. On July 25, 1952, Puerto Rico became a commonwealth with its own constitution approved by the Congress on July 1. This gave the island self-government under a constitution ratified by Puerto Ricans on March 3 of that year. Puerto Ricans have a nonvoting delegate in Congress, and they cannot vote in presidential elections.

In 1960, President John F. Kennedy and Governor Luis Muñoz Marin agreed that the people of Puerto Rico could choose statehood, independence, or remain a commonwealth. Although the island is still a commonwealth, this is not the wish of all Puerto Ricans, many of whom want independence. But because Puerto Rico needs millions of dollars every year from the United States to survive, the independence of the island now is economically impossible. Only 20 percent of the citizens want independence; the rest are almost equally divided between remaining a commonwealth or becoming a state.

EDUCATION

Until 1948, the U.S. government was in charge of education in Puerto Rico, and classes were taught in English. Since most children spoke only Spanish, this made learning difficult. Then, the U.S. government gave Puerto Rico the job of educating its children, and classes were taught in Spanish with English as a required subject. Students learned faster in their native language, and many parents who had kept their children out of school sent them to classes. This increase in school attendance has given Puerto Rico a better educated population than it had before 1948.

Children in Puerto Rico are required to attend school. However, a small number in isolated villages do not go to classes because they live too far from a school. In addition to public schools, there are privately owned schools and schools administered by churches. The island also has three universities: the University of Puerto Rico, Inter-American University, and Catholic University. There are also smaller colleges on the island that specialize in business, electronics, and technology.

SPORTS

Puerto Ricans like sports, especially baseball, basketball, swimming, and horse racing. They also consider cockfighting a sport. In cockfighting, roosters trained to fight with spurs attached to their legs are put in a closed area called a cockpit and they fight until one of them dies or is too crippled to continue. Cockfighting is illegal in the United States.

HOLIDAYS AND FESTIVALS

Puerto Rico observes the same holidays that are celebrated in the fifty states. The Puerto Ricans also have fiestas to commemorate feast days according to the calendar of the Catholic Church. Each town has a patron saint, and residents honor their saint's feast day every year with special mass services. After these services, worshipers carry a statue or a relic of the saint through the streets of the city or village, and then hold day-long and sometimes week-long festivals. The largest celebration of a saint's day is the Feast of St. John the Baptist, which is observed for days before and after June 24, the actual feast day. On June 23, some families stay up all night on the beach. When the sun comes up, they wade into the water to relive the baptism of Christ by John the Baptist.

Christmas is a month-long celebration that begins early in December and ends January 6. Gifts are exchanged on Christmas Eve (Nochebuena) and on Three Kings' Day (Epiphany), January 6. Santa Claus brings presents on Christmas Eve, but for Three Kings' Day, children put grass under their beds for the camels of the Magi. In the morning, toys and candy have replaced the grass, and children believe that the Magi left the presents in exchange for grass for their camels.

ANIMALS AND PLANTS

There are no poisonous snakes, insects, or dangerous animals in Puerto Rico. Mongooses, which were brought to the island years ago to control rats and snakes on sugar cane plantations, keep the rat and nonpoisonous snake population under control, but there are many mosquitoes, flies, and mimis or sand fleas.

The environment on the island is excellent for turtles, iguanas, bats, and the coqui, a small tree frog that can cling upside down to tree leaves and change color as protection from the sun and its enemies. But except for domesticated animals such as oxen, cattle, hogs, dogs, and cats, there are few animals in Puerto Rico.

Over 180 species of birds have been sighted on the island. Many are migratory, but about thirty species are native to the island. The island bird is the reinita, a warbler with a gray head and a yellow body. It likes sugar so

Puerto Ricans gather in the narrow streets of old San Juan to celebrate.

much it is sometimes called "sugar bird." Some people put saucers filled with sugar on their windowsills; this not only feeds the birds, it keeps them from flying into the houses in search of sugar.

Over 3,000 species of plants, trees, shrubs, and flowers grow in Puerto Rico. The major crop plants are sugar cane, tobacco, coffee, and fruits. Oranges, mangoes, avocados, papayas, bananas, pineapples, guavas, and breadfruit grow wild, as do bamboo, palms, ferns, hibiscus, poinsettias, jasmine, orchids, lilies, and carnations. The island tree is the ceiba, a small tree with crimson and scarlet flowers. The island flower is the maga.

As you can see from the preceding description, there are many differences and similarities between Puerto Rico and the United States.

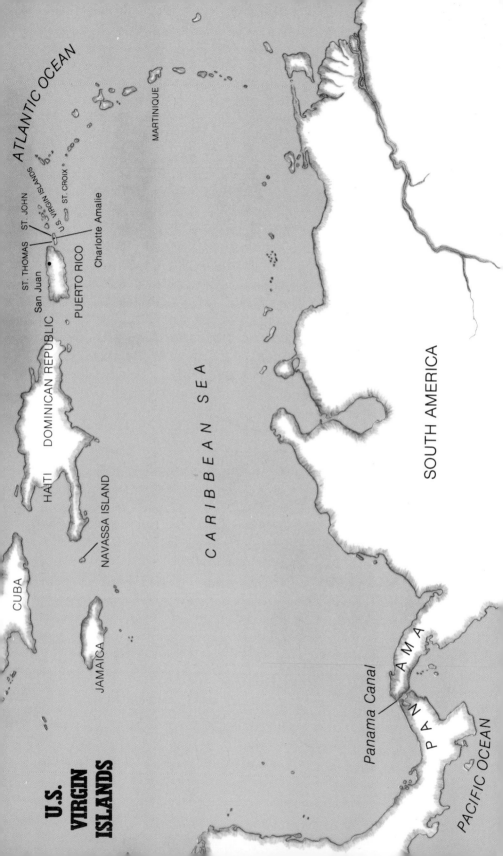

THREE

THE U.S. VIRGIN ISLANDS

The U.S. Virgin Islands, like Puerto Rico, are peaks of mountains that sank below the water millions of years ago. They have a land area of 132 square miles (550 sq. km), which includes more than fifty islets and the main islands of St. Thomas, St. Croix, and St. John. The Virgin Islands are 70 miles (115 km) east of Puerto Rico. There is also a group of islands owned by Great Britain, known as the British Virgin Islands. However, in this book the Virgin Islands refer to the U.S. Virgin Islands. About 102,000 people live in the Virgin Islands. The capital is Charlotte Amalie on St. Thomas.

DISCOVERY AND COLONIZATION

It is believed that the Virgin Islands were first settled hundreds of thousands of years ago by Carib Indians from South America. Christopher Columbus discovered the islands in 1493, during his second voyage to the New World, and called them the Virgin Islands.

When Columbus went ashore, he was met by Carib Indians with poisoned arrows. One of his ships rammed the Indian canoe, but the Indians, led by a woman, kept shooting their arrows. Some Indians were finally captured and brought to Spain. By 1596 the Indians were gone: some had been killed by pirates, some were killed by Spaniards, whereas others had left the islands, unable to defend themselves with their primitive weapons.

The islands were mostly uninhabited until 1625, when British, French, and Dutch citizens arrived within a short time of each other to settle St. Croix. As these settlers tried to extend their claims for land, fights broke out. When an island war began between the British and the Dutch, the French sided with the Dutch. The British won the conflict, and the Dutch and French eventually left the island.

On August 10, 1650, 1,200 Spanish soldiers from Puerto Rico invaded St. Croix, massacred more than 100 British settlers, and forced the others to leave. The Spaniards held the island only a few months. When the Dutch heard that the British were gone, they tried to take the island but were defeated. The French attacked shortly after and took the island.

During the years of fighting for St. Croix, groups of French, Dutch, Danes, and British came to St. Thomas. Most of them could not establish profitable farms on the hilly terrain, and they left. In 1665, a plan to colonize St. Thomas was approved by Frederick III, the king of Denmark. However, the settlement was ravaged by sickness, pirates, and a hurricane. After nineteen months, the surviving Danes abandoned the island, which they had called the Danish West Indies.

The Danish West Indies and Guinea Company arrived from Denmark on May 25, 1672, to try once again to settle St. Thomas. They built a colony on the southern coast and called it Charlotte Amalie in honor of Denmark's queen. They quickly learned what earlier settlers had learned: the island was too hilly for good farming.

The Danish company might have abandoned the island, too, if John Lorenz had not arrived to help the settlement make money. Lorenz's way of making money was to talk the Danish company into bringing Africans to St. Thomas. The slaves dug and then planted the hills with sugar cane, and the Danish company made so much money it went looking for more land.

The Danish company had claimed St. John in 1688, but colonists had been driven off by pirates and invaders from other countries. In 1717, the Danes built and manned a fort on St. John and the invasions stopped. The planted hills of St. Thomas and St. John created a large profit for the Danish company, and it offered to buy St. Croix from France. The French colony had been attacked several times by the British and the Dutch and made little profit from the island. The French agreed to sell St. Croix to Denmark in 1733.

In November of that year, slaves seized the fort on St. John and signaled other slaves to rebel by firing three cannon shots. The slaves burned houses and sugar factories. The governor of St. Thomas learned of the revolt from a man who had escaped from the fort. The governor sent soldiers to St. John, but the slaves fought so hard the soldiers could not land.

The slaves held the island for six months. To regain control, the governor asked for help from the French on Martinique, an island southeast of the Virgin Islands. If the French would help, their reward would be slaves. The French were able to land on St. John, and on May 24,

1734, with their ammunition gone, more than 300 slaves committed suicide. Some of the slaves who did not commit suicide were given to the French and others were executed. Further attempts at freedom through revolt were made. But it was the work of Governor-General Peter Carl von Scholten over a number of years that led to a declaration of emancipation of all the slaves in 1848.

In January 1865, U.S. Secretary of State William H. Seward began negotiations with Denmark to buy the Virgin Islands. But the assassination of President Abraham Lincoln and the wounding of Seward delayed the negotiations until 1867. These negotiations were further delayed by the impeachment proceedings of President Andrew Johnson. Talks continued on and off until the beginning of World War I and the opening of the Panama Canal in 1914.

The United States feared that the Germans might conquer Denmark and, as a result, own the Virgin Islands. This would put German-owned land close to the Panama Canal, an important shipping passage between the Atlantic and Pacific oceans. The United States had rights to the canal and wanted to keep them.

The United States opened serious talks with Denmark, and on January 16, 1917, President Woodrow Wilson signed a treaty to buy the Virgin Islands. On March

More than three hundred years later, harvesting sugar cane is still an important part of the Virgin Islands' industry. Here, the cane is being unloaded at a mill.

31 of that year, Denmark transferred the ownership of the Virgin Islands to the United States. Six days later, the United States entered World War I in a good position to defend the Panama Canal, although this did not become necessary.

U.S. TERRITORY

For a number of years, Denmark had neglected the Virgin Islands. When the United States took them over, they found the people in desperate need of food and healthy water. The filthy hospitals created a high death rate, and schools were run down. The islands were put under military rule until the United States could decide how to help the residents.

Under the U. S. Department of the Navy, the islands' hospitals were reorganized, nurses were trained, people were vaccinated against smallpox, and sanitation projects were begun. But the Americans seemed less enthusiastic about helping the people support themselves. They ignored hundreds of years of island culture and created resentment by their treatment of black citizens.

Although the islanders appreciated the improvements in their lives, they resented the Americans. They also resented not having any say in their own government. The islanders felt that when the American flag went up on the islands in 1917, they should have become citizens of the United States. Instead, it took ten years to achieve that goal. On January 17, 1927, all natives of the Virgin Islands were proclaimed citizens of the United States. On February 27, 1931, the islands were transferred from the Department of the Navy to the Department of the Interior.

GROWTH AND INDUSTRY

After the Department of the Interior took over the islands, President Woodrow Wilson called them the "poorhouse of the United States." During the navy's rule, sugar prices had dropped and droughts plagued the islands. This caused factories to close and thousands of workers were put out of work. Many people were near starvation, and the death rate for children, which had dropped shortly after the United States bought the islands, rose again. People hoped that the transfer from military to civilian government would make the islands self-supporting.

The first civilian governor of the Virgin Islands was Paul M. Pearson. When he saw the living conditions on the islands, he pushed for economic reforms, which created opposition from Washington politicians who did not like his requests for additional help for the people. Governor Pearson continued to ask, and by the time he left the island in 1935, he had given residents more responsibility in their government. He had also improved the schools and social and economic conditions on the islands.

The Virgin Islands Company began under Governor Pearson's administration. He called the company a partnership program between the U.S. government and the Virgin Islands. The company increased the use of the limited land, built houses, developed transportation, and promoted tourism.

All this created jobs and a better life for the citizens. Another reason for the improvement in conditions on the islands was a decline in the population. In the mid-1930s, there were fewer people on the islands than there had been when Denmark transferred their ownership to the United States. The main reason for this decline was the large number of people who left the islands to find work in the United States before the Virgin Islands Company was formed.

After the company started, most workers on the islands were able to find jobs. Additional jobs were created when an air base and a submarine base were built on St. Thomas. Then, during World War II, an air base was built on St. Croix. There were not enough workers on the Virgin Islands to fill these jobs and harvest the sugar cane so people were brought in from other islands to fill these job opportunities.

After the war, the military bases closed but many of the people from other areas remained in the Virgin Islands. This caused temporary high unemployment. However, the growing tourist industry created new jobs. Today, the tourist industry employs so many workers that more people have come from other islands to fill the need.

In addition to tourism, there are oil refineries and textile manufacturing and watch assembly facilities on the islands, but industrial growth is limited by lack of land and water. The islands have no permanent streams or underground water. Desalination plants have made it possible for a number of businesses to operate, but nothing can be done about the limited amount of land. This means that much of the food, clothing, fuel, and medicine used by the Virgin Islands must be imported from the United States.

GOVERNMENT

After the Virgin Islands were transferred to the United States and placed under the Department of the Navy, the commander of the naval fleet stationed at St. Thomas served as governor of the islands. On January 30, 1931,

*A tourist resort surrounded by mountains
and palm trees on the Virgin Islands*

*Although industry on the Virgin Islands
is limited, this aluminum plant is an
example of the variety of industry
found on the islands.*

with the transfer of the islands to the Department of the Interior, Paul M. Pearson became the first civilian governor.

Pearson was white, as were all governors who followed him until 1946 when William H. Hastie became the first black governor. This was a major victory for the islanders who are 85 percent black. The islanders won another victory on September 25, 1958, when John Merwin became the first native-born governor. But these men were appointed by the President of the United States who had appointed all governors to the islands. Finally in 1970, Melvin H. Evans, the first governor elected by the people of the islands, took office.

The islanders have a nonvoting representative in the U.S. Congress, and they cannot vote in presidential elections. However, the majority of the people of the Virgin Islands say they are satisfied with their present form of government.

EDUCATION

Classes in the Virgin Islands are taught in English, and children between the ages of five-and-one-half and sixteen are required to attend school. In addition to the public schools, there are privately owned schools and schools administered by churches.

Until 1963, there was no college on the islands, but that year, the College of the Virgin Islands opened, and it now has campuses on St. Thomas and St. Croix.

HOLIDAYS AND FESTIVALS

Residents of the Virgin Islands commemorate the same national holidays as people who live in the United States.

They also celebrate Emancipation Day on July 3 to commemorate the day in 1848 when the slaves were freed. July 23 is Supplication Day when people say prayers to ask protection from hurricanes during the coming hurricane season. The islanders also celebrate the annual carnivals on St. Thomas and St. John and the Crucian Christmas Fiesta on St. Croix.

The carnival on St. Thomas is held from April 30 to May 5. The origin of this celebration goes back to the arrival of African slaves, and many dances are derived from African native dances. Over the years, the carnival has developed into a week-long celebration. People organize dance troupes and steel bands, and make costumes and build floats. Schools and community groups hold contests to choose their entries for carnival queen and king. People write music for the carnival song. All week there are parties, and the carnival ends with the *J'Ouvert Morning Tramp*. This is a predawn dance through the streets with *Mocko Jumbies*, the traditional symbol of the carnival. Mocko Jumbies are people who prance around on 17-foot (5-m) stilts wearing brightly colored clothes covered with mirrors.

The carnival on St. John, held on July 4th, is celebrated with parades, floats, and costumes. The Crucian Christmas Fiesta on St. Croix is a two-week celebration that begins on December 23 and ends on January 6, Three Kings' Day. January 6 is the Feast of the Epiphany in the Christian calendar, and the observance is similar to the carnivals on St. Thomas and St. John with Christmas carols added.

FLORA AND FAUNA

The Virgin Islands National Park, dedicated in 1956, covers almost two-thirds of St. John and includes 5,650 acres

*The St. Croix Christmas Carnival,
complete with costumes and masks*

(2,260 ha) of water. The underwater portion of the park and the land area cover 15,000 acres (6,000 ha). It is the smallest U.S. national park.

In the waters are brain, star, staghorn, elkhorn, and fan coral. Around and in the coral are hawksbill turtles, sponges, eels, and sea urchins. The most common fish in the park waters are yellowtail snappers, foureye butterflyfish, squirrelfish, and parrotfish. Dolphins play off shore and humpbacked whales visit during mating season. Land hermit crabs, small lizards, mongooses, and bats also live in the park. Bats are the only native mammals on St. John.

Petroglyphs mark some of the cliffs. People believed that these rock carvings were made before Columbus came to the Virgin Islands, but recent studies show that some of these carvings are similar to designs of African cultures and may date from early slave days on the island. Also in the park are ruins of a sugar mill, which is a reminder of the work the slaves did.

Except for a small number of deer and wild boar, there are no large animals on the islands. The official bird of the three islands is the yellow breast. There are over 220 species of birds on the islands including parrots, pelicans, and doves.

The territorial flower is the yellow elder, also known as ginger thomas. Other flowers found throughout the islands include bougainvillea, hibiscus, orchids, oleander, poinsettia, and bird of paradise.

Trees include African tulip, seagrape, mahogany, and several kinds of palms. There are also mango, papaya, peach, banana, pineapple, pear, and breadfruit trees.

In 1493, Christopher Columbus wrote in his diary that the islands were mountainous and very green down to the sea. When the Danes established their plantations, forests were cleared for sugar cane and cotton fields. This destroyed much of what Columbus had written as being "delightful to see." When slavery ended, plantations were abandoned, and the land was left to restore itself. If Columbus were alive today, he would again think the islands were delightful to see.

COMMONWEALTH OF THE NORTHERN MARIANAS AND THE FREELY ASSOCIATED STATES

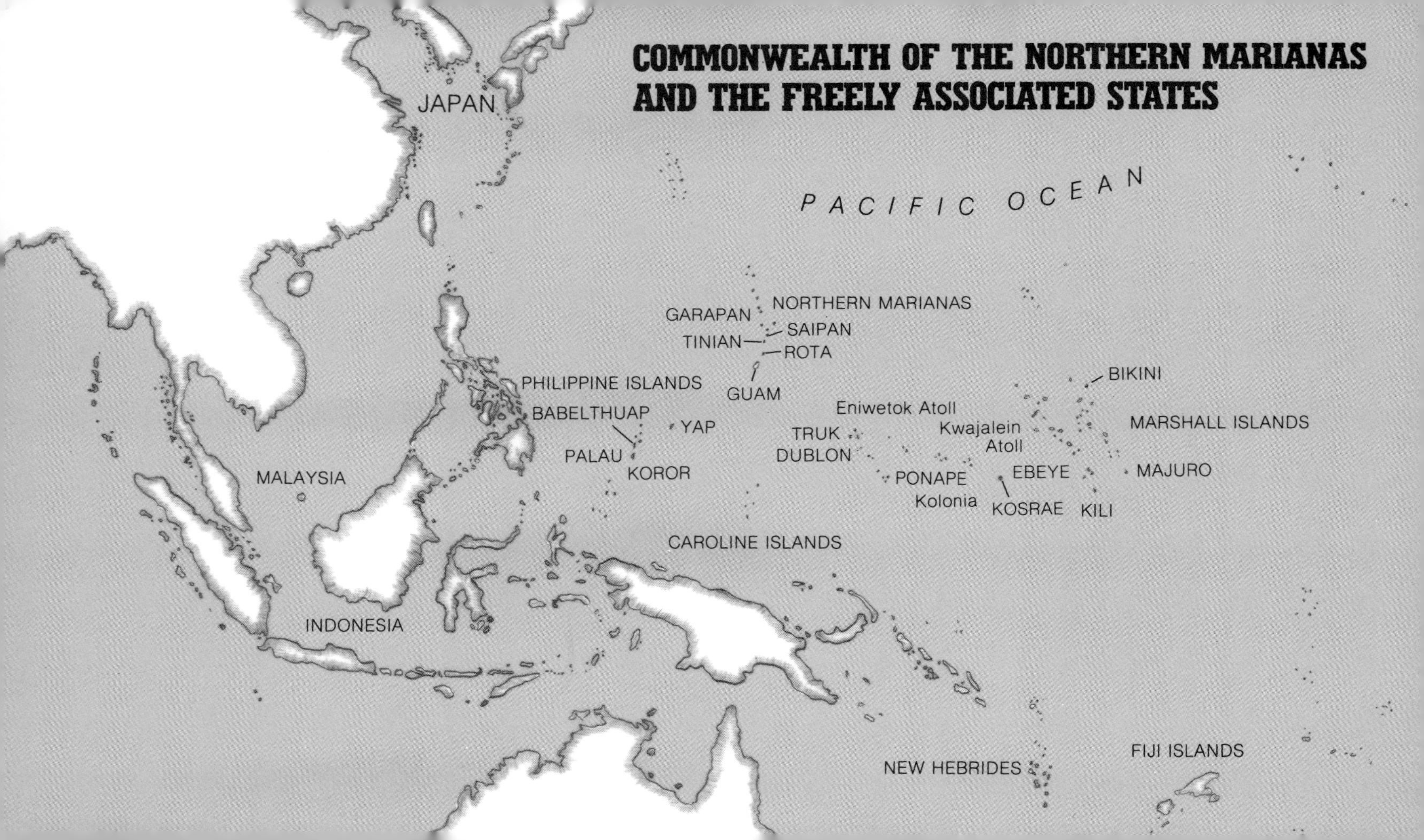

PACIFIC OCEAN

JAPAN

PHILIPPINE ISLANDS

MALAYSIA

INDONESIA

GARAPAN NORTHERN MARIANAS
TINIAN — SAIPAN
ROTA
GUAM

Eniwetok Atoll

BABELTHUAP
YAP
PALAU
KOROR

TRUK
DUBLON

CAROLINE ISLANDS

BIKINI

MARSHALL ISLANDS

Kwajalein
Atoll
EBEYE
Kolonia KOSRAE KILI
PONAPE
MAJURO

NEW HEBRIDES

FIJI ISLANDS

FOUR

THE COMMONWEALTH OF THE NORTHERN MARIANAS AND THE FREELY ASSOCIATED STATES

The 2,141 islands that form the Trust Territory are collectively known as Micronesia, which means "small islands." Most of these are so small that only about 100 of the 2,141 islands are inhabited. Today, these islands are called freely associated states. The islands are scattered throughout the Pacific Ocean over an area as large as the continental United States. But if the land masses of all these islands were lumped together they would cover only two-thirds of Rhode Island, the smallest state.

From 1947 to 1986, the United States administered Micronesia for the United Nations. On maps, these islands form an imperfect "U." The Northern Marianas run north to south on the western part of the "U," and the Carolines run west to east on the bottom of the "U." The Marshalls run from south to north on the eastern part of the "U." About 120,500 people live in these islands.

DISCOVERY AND
COLONIZATION

It is believed that the islands were settled about 1,000 B.C., by people from Malaysia in southeast Asia. These settlers had little contact with people from other parts of the world until 1521, when Ferdinand Magellan stopped on Guam during his trip around the world for Spain.

For more than a century, Spain was the dominant country in Micronesia but it did little for the natives. However, despite this disinterest, the Spaniards insisted that traders from other nations stop at the Philippines, which Spain also owned, to buy a permit before trading with the islanders. Germany did not obey the order, and Pope Leo XIII was asked to settle the conflict. The Pope recognized Spain's claim to Micronesia, but he granted Germany the right to trade and fish without permits.

The Germans were not satisfied with this. For a number of years, they had been settling on the islands and they did not stop. This brought continuing disagreements between Spain and Germany that did not end until 1898, when Spain lost the Spanish-American War. Unable to afford or defend Micronesia, Spain sold most of the islands to the German Empire for $4.5 million.

The Germans were determined to make money from the islands. They forced the native residents to work for little pay. They also ordered male adults to work fifteen days out of every year for the government. If they resisted, they were killed or exiled from their islands and families. During World War I, Germany lost the islands, and after the war the League of Nations named Japan as the administrator of Micronesia.

The Japanese hoped to ease the overpopulation in their country by colonizing Micronesia. By the end of the

1930s, thousands of Japanese lived on the islands. They had built roads, shrines, and homes, and established businesses and farms.

These colonization and building activities were acceptable to the League of Nations. What was not acceptable to the organization was Japan's fortification of the islands. In violation of the League of Nations agreement, the Japanese secretly built military bases from which they launched their attack on Pearl Harbor, in Hawaii, on December 7, 1941. For four years, the United States fought its way across the Pacific to reach Japan. By New Year's Day 1945, almost everything the Japanese had built in Micronesia had been destroyed by bombings from U.S. planes.

UNITED NATIONS
TRUSTEESHIP

When the war ended, the United Nations assigned the Caroline Islands, the Marshall Islands, and the Northern Mariana Islands to the United States.

The Trust Territory Code said that the natives would have religious freedom; would receive education, health care, and economic aid; and would eventually be given the opportunity to decide their political future. To make the islands easier to administer, they were divided into six districts: the Northern Marianas, the Marshalls, and Paulau, Ponape, Truk, and Yap in the Carolines.

There was no problem with religious freedom. The natives were allowed to worship any god they believed in and in any language they preferred. But most islanders had their own languages or dialects, and natives found it difficult to communicate among themselves. In addition, the people had been forced to learn several languages over the years. Under Spain's rule if they did not speak Spanish, they were beaten. The Germans brought their language, and the Japanese, who hoped to make the islands part of their empire, insisted that the natives speak Japanese.

After World War II, the solution to the communication problem was to make English the official language of Micronesia, while allowing the natives to speak their own dialects. It was a good solution but difficult to implement. Few people on the islands could speak English well enough to teach it, and teachers who traveled to the islands from the United States faced students who could not understand them. Still, temporary buildings were put up to serve as schools, and the educational condition of the trusteeship moved forward.

Health services were also difficult to arrange. Doctors and nurses were few, and supplies of medicine were scarce. The United States solved the supply problem by shipping medicines by airplane, but medical personnel remained hard to find. Like schools, medical facilities were housed in temporary buildings, and health services were provided.

The United States made one decision about Micronesia that practically stopped progress on the islands. The United States decided to leave economic development to the Micronesians and to let them run the businesses so they could become financially independent. It was an unselfish idea, but it was not workable.

For most of their lives, the natives had lived off the land and the sea. People on the smaller islands could still do this. However, during the Japanese colonization, many people on the larger islands had stopped their subsistence living. The Japanese had created jobs and many residents depended on them. In addition, much of the natural food growth on which the Micronesians had depended all their lives had been destroyed during World War II.

By 1962, there had been so little economic growth on the islands that the United States abandoned its hope for economic independence for Micronesia. That year, President John F. Kennedy urged that foreign businesses be allowed to operate on the islands and that the islanders be encouraged to move toward self-government.

On January 19, 1965, the islanders held an election to choose candidates for a newly formed organization called the Congress of Micronesia. In the summer of 1965, the winners of the election held a meeting on Saipan, which lies about 3,700 miles (5,900 km) west of Hawaii and is the largest island in the Northern Marianas. This first meeting of the congress was a giant step toward self-government for the Caroline, Marshall, and Northern Mariana islands.

SELF-GOVERNMENT

In 1970, the United States offered commonwealth status to the people of Micronesia, but their leaders turned down the offer. However, the citizens of the Northern Marianas wanted to become a commonwealth, and they began separate negotiations with the United States. On June 17, 1975, they voted to establish a commonwealth of the Northern Marianas. President Gerald Ford signed an agreement on March 24, 1976. More than ten years later, on November 3, 1986, after the passage of Public Law 94–241, the Northern Marianas officially became a part of the United States, and the residents became U.S. citizens. Admiral James Lyons, Jr., the Pacific Fleet commander, gave Governor Pedro Toniaro the first U.S. passport during the ceremony held on Saipan.

Kosrae in the Caroline Islands replaced Saipan as

one of the six districts of the Trust Territory. On July 12, 1978, voters in the Marshall Islands and the districts of Kosrae, Palau, Ponape, Truk, and Yap voted on a proposed constitution, which was approved in Kosrae, Ponape, Truk, and Yap, but not approved by the Marshall Islands and Palau. The constitution became effective in Kosrae, Ponape, Truk, and Yap on May 10, 1979. These four districts became the Federated States of Micronesia. Each district is a state with an elected governor. Kolonia on Ponape is the capital of the Federated States.

On May 1, 1979, the people of the Marshall Islands approved a constitution modeled after the government of New Zealand and became the Republic of the Marshall Islands. Majuro is its capital. The Palau District ratified its constitution on July 9, 1980. It is now the Republic of Palau with Koror as its capital.

Voters in the Federated States of Micronesia, the Republic of the Marshall Islands, and the Republic of Palau have agreed to a Compact of Free Association with the United States. The agreement gives the islands self-government and economic help from the United States. In return for the economic help, the United States has the right to build and control military and defense activities and has the responsibility to defend the islands against military invasion. The United Nations has released the islands from the United Nations Trust, which had been in effect since 1947.

EVERYDAY FOOD

The islands have a warm, tropical climate. There are two seasons, wet and dry. Rain falls during the dry season from January to June, but it is not as frequent or as heavy as it is in the rainy season from July to December. Occasionally typhoons pass through the area during the rainy season.

Because of the similar climate on the islands, most have similar plants that supply much of their food. Some islands have papayas, apples, and mangoes. Almost all have breadfruit, taro, sweet potatoes, bananas, and coconuts.

The coconut tree is the most valuable tree for the islands. The meat from the nuts is sweet and nutritious. The nuts also give "milk," which is what the liquid in coconuts is often called. The leaves are used to make roofs, walls, and mats for floors. The fiber from the husk is soaked in water until the fibers separate. Then they are dried and woven to make rope. This rope ties the beams and pillars for houses, which are sometimes built from coconut tree trunks. Thread made from ribs of the leaves is used to weave fishing nets. The use of the coconut tree that contributes most to the economy of the islands is copra, which is the dried meat of the coconut that is used to make margarine, cooking oil, soap, and cosmetics.

INDUSTRY

Copra and fish products are the main exports of the islands. Other exports are shells and handicrafts. There is little private industry and much of what the residents use is imported. Tourism, however, has developed small businesses and created jobs. But this is not enough to support these islands in the Pacific, and they must rely largely on financial aid from the United States for their needs.

THE NORTHERN MARIANAS

The fourteen islands that form the Northern Marianas are the peaks of a volcanic mountain range that rises more than 30,000 feet (9,150 m) from the bottom of the ocean. Most of the residents live on Saipan, Tinian, and Rota. The remaining islands have a population of about only 100 people. The natives are called *Chamorros*, and latte stone pillars made with coral limestone are reminders of people who lived on the islands before Spain claimed them. Today, about 18,000 people live in the Northern Marianas whose capital is Garapan.

Spain sold the islands to Germany in 1899. After Germany's defeat in World War I, the Japanese administered the islands. They built a sugar cane processing center and a small railroad to move the processed sugar by ships. The Japanese, as noted, also secretly fortified the islands to launch their attack on Pearl Harbor, which began World War II.

Today, a red engine that was once used to haul the cane stands in Sugar King Park in Garapan as a reminder of Saipan's peaceful days. Battle sites have also been preserved to show where thousands of Americans and Japanese died during the bombings and invasions of the islands. When civilian Japanese saw that the Americans would capture Saipan, hundreds of them jumped to their deaths rather than face capture by the Americans. A monument stands in their memory at Bonzai Cliff on the northern tip of Saipan.

Coconut trees, so valuable
to the islanders,
on the Marshall Islands

The taking of the Marianas by the United States cracked the Japanese defense in the Pacific, and Saipan and Tinian became take-off points for planes on bombing missions to Japan. On August 6, 1945, a B-29 called the *Enola Gay* left Tinian to drop an atomic bomb on the city of Hiroshima. The damage to Hiroshima followed by the bombing of Nagasaki was so devastating that Japan surrendered to the United States shortly after these attacks, and World War II ended.

After the war, the United States took over the administration of the islands under the Department of the Navy. In 1950, all the Northern Marianas except Saipan were turned over to the Department of the Interior. When the Department of the Navy continued to hold Saipan, the United Nations asked the United States why the military still held the island. After years of prodding by the United Nations, the United States turned Saipan over to the Department of the Interior in 1962.

The navy's reason for holding the island was a Central Intelligence Agency (CIA) training village built in the central area of Saipan. There, the CIA conducted a supersecret project to prepare Chinese Nationalist troops to invade the mainland of China and retake the country. When the training was discontinued, the buildings the navy had built for that project became the Trust Territory Headquarters. The headquarters are now the office buildings for the Commonwealth of the Northern Marianas.

THE CAROLINE ISLANDS

Four of the original six districts of the Trust Territories were in the Caroline Islands: Palau, Ponape, Truk, and Yap. There are more than 930 islands in the Caroline

Islands. Some rise only a few feet out of the ocean. These are called "low" or "coral islands." The rest are "high islands," which are peaks of volcanic mountains that rise 2,000 feet (610 m) from the bottom of the ocean. About 80,000 people live in the Caroline Islands.

PONAPE

Ponape has remnants of three previous rulers of Micronesia: a Spanish fort, an agricultural station that was started by the Germans, and a fortification built by the Japanese. But the most unusual reminder of the past is Nan Madol.

Long before the Spaniards made Ponape their headquarters in Micronesia, settlers had erected a kingdom on the southeast coast of Ponape. Archaeologists believe that the palace, ceremonial halls, temples, forts, and burial places of Nan Madol were built in the early thirteenth century by the Saudeleurs, a dynasty of Ponape rulers.

With only human labor to move slabs of basalt stone, the Saudeleurs created a kingdom where they lived in luxury for generations. When the ancestors of the modern Ponapeans invaded Nan Madol, the Saudeleurs were not strong enough to stop them. No one knows for certain whether the Saudeleurs were killed or allowed to leave.

Because people on Ponape believed that ghosts lived in Nan Madol, they let the jungle grow over it. The Japanese cleared some of the trees and shrubs, but after they left, the jungle buried the city again because many people still believed in the ghosts. With more and more travelers visiting Ponape, some of Nan Madol has been cleared and it has become a tourist attraction.

Ponape was almost untouched by World War II. Although the island was bombed, it was not heavily damaged and it was never invaded by the Americans.

TRUK

Millions of years ago, Truk was a large island. When it sank into the ocean, its eleven highest peaks were caught in and around the world's biggest lagoon, a shallow body of water near a larger body of water. At its widest point, the lagoon is almost 40 miles (64 km) across.

Japan maintained its headquarters on Dublon, one of the islands in the lagoon, and its largest fleet of ships outside of Japan was anchored there. By 1944, most of the Japanese fleet had left, but more than sixty ships were sunk during raids by American planes. The ships, which are still at the bottom of the lagoon, are designated as an underwater memorial park and nothing may be removed from them. Dublon still has remains of homes, shops, and schools used by the more than 40,000 Japanese who lived there.

YAP

Yap was the smallest district of the Trust Territory. It was not heavily damaged during World War II, but thousands

Top: *basalt stones and jungle growth characterize Nan Madol, known as the "Venice of the Pacific" because it is accessible only by small boat or canoe.* Bottom: *villagers walking in the Ponape countryside.*

of pieces of Yap's stone money, called *rai*, were ground up during the war to pave roads and airstrips and to use as anchors for ships. The loss of their coins was difficult for the people of Yap. The money was valuable to buy food, boats, and houses. But more important to the Yapanese, the coins were also part of their heritage.

Hundreds of years ago, the ancestors of the Yaps had traveled 300 miles (480 km) in canoes across the ocean to Palau to quarry aragonite and calcite. It was not unusual for twenty canoes to leave Yap and to have only one return. Therefore, the more dangerous the trip, the greater was the value of the doughnut-shaped coins.

The people of Yap now have modern money, but this does not lessen their love for their ancient coins, which are from 6 inches (15 cm) to 12 feet (365 cm) across and can weigh several tons. Each coin has a hole in the center so a pole can be poked through it and carried by several people.

Small coins are kept in houses, but large ones are kept outside. Although ownership passes from one person to another, the large coins are not moved. The largest coins often belong to a village. If people in the village buy something with their coin, it stays in the village where it was originally deposited by the long-ago Yapanese. But everyone knows that ownership has changed.

PALAU

The largest island of the Palau Island group is Babelthuap, which was also the largest island in the Trust Ter-

Stone money, called rai, *in front of a grocery store on Yap Island*

ritory. However, most of the people live on the island of Koror.

The city of Koror was named for the island and is now the capital of Palau. It used to be the capital of the Japanese Empire in Micronesia. The Japanese had developed such a beautiful city that it became a vacation resort for wealthy people of Japan who wanted to get away for the winter. The city also had a pineapple industry, fish canneries, and smaller businesses that provided jobs for Palauans. Laborers were brought in from Japan, Korea, and Okinawa. Almost everything was destroyed during the bombing by American planes during World War II.

After the United States began administering Palau for the United Nations, the surviving strips of paved streets built by the Japanese became filled with potholes. Vines grew over the sidewalks, and the cement foundations from the prewar buildings were covered with salvaged lumber and corrugated iron sheeting. Even the coconut trees, which had covered the island since the first natives arrived on Palau, were gone.

In 1942, beetles infested the islands and killed half of the coconut trees. The rest were destroyed by the Japanese to make an airfield and later by bombs from American planes. After the war, only the hibiscus, bougainvillea, and gardenias blooming throughout the city gave hope that Koror would be beautiful again.

Today, Koror has homes, churches, schools, hospitals, a boatyard, fish-freezing facilities, an office of tourism, an agriculture station, a scientific laboratory, and a museum. Near the museum is a reconstructed *Abai*, which is a clubhouse, with a peaked, thatched roof. The gables are decorated with Palauan paintings and storyboards that give the legends and the history of the islands in picture carvings.

THE MARSHALL ISLANDS

The Marshall Islands have 1,136 individual islands that form two chains that line up parallel to each other. The Rabak Group on the east is called Sunrise and the Ralik Group on the west is called Sunset. These two chains are about 150 miles (240 km) apart and are spread over an area twice the size of Texas with only 70 square miles (292 sq km) of land. There are about 31,000 people in the Marshall Islands.

Because the Marshallese have so little land, their land is especially important to them. Despite this, the United States took some of their land. Shortly after World War II ended, the people of Bikini were evacuated to another island so the United States could conduct atomic bomb tests. After a year, the natives complained that there were not enough fish and crops on the new island to feed them adequately.

Since Bikini was still radioactive from the atomic testing, the U.S. government settled the Bikinians on Kili. Some of them returned to Bikini after the U.S. government said the radiation was at a safe level. But when the Energy and Development Administration sent investigators to the island, they found it still had dangerous levels of radiation. The people who had returned were resettled once again.

These resettlements have caused resentment and feelings of homelessness among Bikinians. The people live in overcrowded conditions and are dependent on the United States government for their food. They want to return to their homes and the self-sufficient life they had on Bikini. Because of the radiation this may never be possible.

The United States also evacuated the Eniwetok atoll, a coral island with a reef surrounding a lagoon, for atomic

*A Bikini family with their belongings
waits to be evacuated to another island.*

bomb tests. During the next eleven years, fifty-three tests including the first hydrogen bomb test were conducted.

A large area of Kwajalein, the biggest atoll in the world, was also taken over by the United States. It became a military base and was developed into an anti-missile installation. The natives did not have to leave their island, but they were crowded into the islet of Ebeye. Conditions were so uncomfortable that President John F. Kennedy ordered the Department of the Interior to improve living conditions. The natives of the three islands received money for their land, but the money did not erase the resentment of many Marshallese.

GUAM

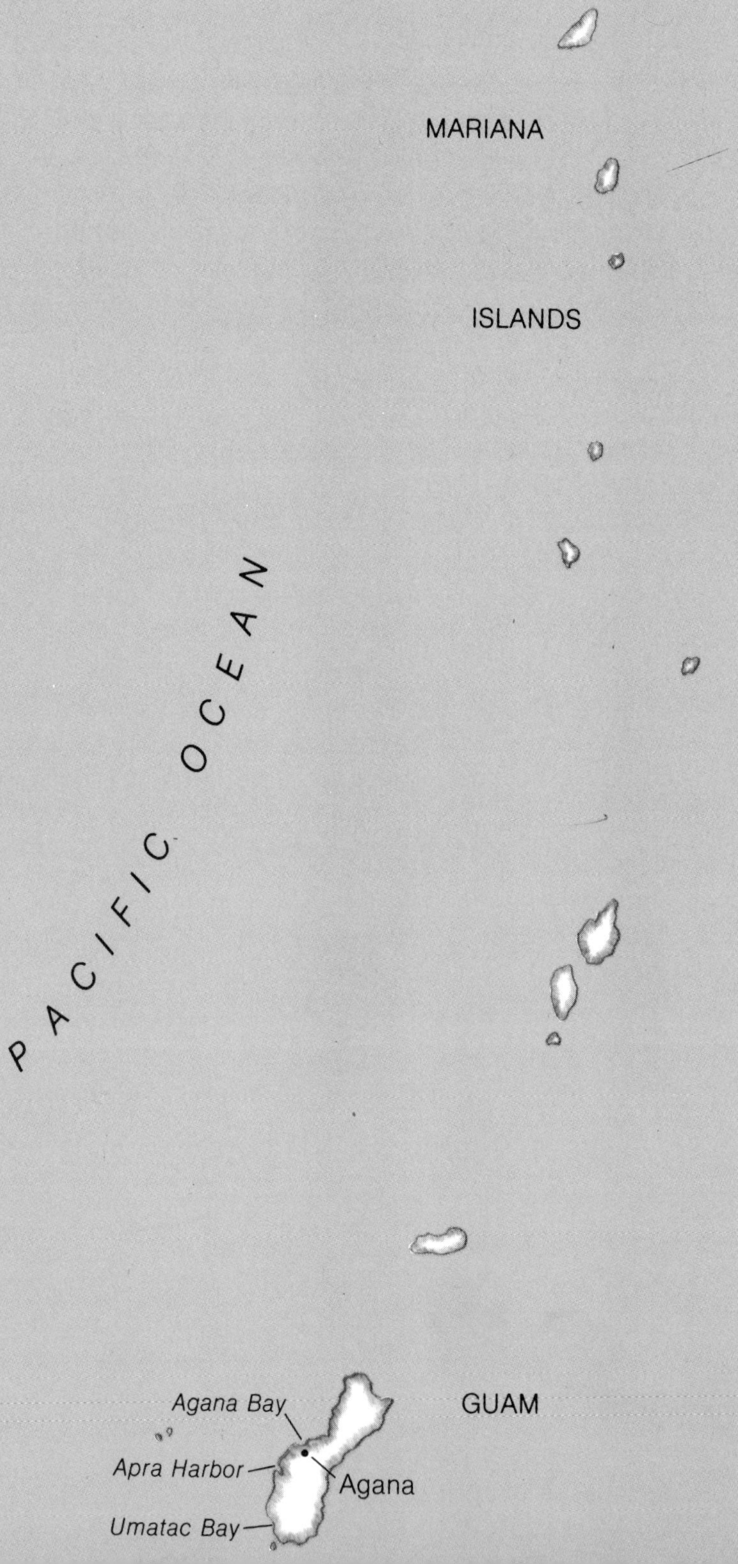

MARIANA

ISLANDS

P A C I F I C   O C E A N

GUAM

Agana Bay

Apra Harbor — Agana

Umatac Bay

FIVE

GUAM

Guam is a volcanic island in the mid-Pacific Ocean 3,700 miles (5,925 km) west of Honolulu, Hawaii. The island is 32 miles (50 km) long, 4 to 8 miles (6 to 12 km) wide, and has 209 square miles (870 sq km) of land. It is part of the Mariana Island chain, but, unlike the other Mariana Islands, Guam was never part of the Trust Territory of the Pacific Islands. About 110,000 people live on Guam. The capital is Agana.

DISCOVERY AND COLONIZATION

Archaeological findings on Guam have revealed artifacts that may date back to 2000 B.C. These artifacts are the oldest found in the western Pacific and indicate that the first people on Guam came from Malaysia or Indonesia and were called *Chamorros*, the same name used for the natives of the Commonwealth of the Northern Marianas. Researchers believe the latte stone pillars made with coral limestone that they built were used to support large houses for groups of families to live in.

The natives had little contact with people from the rest of the world until March 6, 1521, when Magellan stopped at Umatac Bay on the southwestern shore of the island. He named the island *Ladrones*, which means thieves, because he said the natives stole from him.

In 1565, Spain claimed Guam and the other islands of the Marianas. Spanish missionaries came in 1668 and renamed the islands the Marianas in honor of Maria Anna, the queen of Spain. The people of Guam resisted the Spanish. But the Spaniards were well armed and, during the early years, thousands of Chamorros were killed, exiled to other islands, or died from diseases brought to the island by the Spanish and European traders.

THE SPANISH-AMERICAN WAR

The first battle of the Spanish-American War was fought in Manila Bay in the Philippines on April 21, 1898. On April 25, Admiral George Dewey, whose ships were anchored off the China Coast, received orders from the Navy Department to go to the Philippines to capture and destroy the Spanish ships.

When Admiral Dewey arrived, he saw no ships, and on May 1, he sailed into Manila Bay. He found Spanish

Ferdinand Magellan, Portuguese navigator and discoverer of Guam

ships there, and when the battle ended the Spaniards had suffered heavy losses of men and ships. Although Admiral Dewey's sailors suffered few injuries, he did not try to capture Manila. He had no soldiers to hold it, but 10,000 troops were on their way to the Philippines. They were being transported on the *U.S.S. Charleston* and three smaller ships, commanded by Captain Henry Glass.

Captain Glass had orders to capture Guam from the Spanish before he went to the Philippines. Although ready for battle on June 21, he found no ships in Agana Bay and continued south to Apra Harbor. There was no gunfire, but when he spotted Fort Santa Cruz above the harbor, he believed he would be attacked from there.

Captain Glass ordered his men to fire. There was no response from the fort. He anchored and, as he was deciding his plan of attack, a boat approached him with several men. They were taken on board and introduced themselves as customs people ready to collect their fees.

The men thanked Captain Glass for firing his guns to let them know he wished to anchor. They requested the ship's papers and asked Captain Glass the reason for his visit. Captain Glass was surprised to learn the people of Guam didn't know the United States and Spain were at war. After the captain explained his mission, he contacted Governor Juan Marian and requested that he surrender Guam. With only a few soldiers from Spain to defend the island against four American ships, the governor wrote:

". . . Being without defense of any kind and without means for meeting the present situation, I am under the sad necessity of being unable to resist such superior forces and regretfully accede to your demands, at the same time protesting against this act of violence, when

I have received no information from my government to the effect that Spain is in war with your nation."

Captain Glass raised the American flag and the ship's band played "The Star Spangled Banner." Shortly after that ceremony, Captain Glass left Guam to take the American troops to the Philippines.

The Spanish-American War ended on August 12, 1898, less than three months after it began. On December 10, the Treaty of Paris was signed. One of its provisions was to give Guam to the United States.

U.S. TERRITORY

When Captain Glass sailed from Guam, he left the island with no government. With no one in control and only an occasional visit by American ships, some Guamanian leaders tried to establish an independent government. They failed to achieve their goal. On August 7, 1899, more than a year after Captain Glass landed on Guam, the *U.S.S. Yosemite* steamed into Apra Harbor with Captain Richard P. Leary on board. He had been appointed by President William McKinley to become the first American governor of Guam.

Governor Leary had expected to find savages on Guam. Instead, he found gentle people living in conditions he considered deplorable. However, although the Governor's House was less deplorable than the houses in which the Guamanians lived, he said it was not comfortable enough for him. He returned to the *Yosemite* until the Governor's House was cleaned.

When he returned four months later, Governor Leary found the Governor's House painted and repaired. His aide, Lieutenant Edwin Safford, had not only improved the governor's surroundings but had also improved the living conditions in other areas with the help of the Guamanians.

The Agana River, which had been polluted with garbage, had been cleaned; roads were repaired; and farms produced more food. Lieutenant Safford was teaching English three nights a week to anyone who wanted to learn.

Governor Leary was not so helpful. Because he believed the Spanish priests might incite the islanders to rebel against the United States, he expelled them from the island. This left only one native priest to serve 9,000 Catholics. Governor Leary allowed church services, but he banned public religious celebrations and the saints' day processions that were an important part of the culture. When the bells that announced the four o'clock mass every morning disturbed his sleep, the governor ordered the bells silenced. This led to so many problems with the Guamanians that the governor who replaced Governor Leary revoked most of Leary's orders.

The governors were appointed by the President of the United States and they reported to him. Some governors were lenient, whereas others, such as Governor Leary, tried to impose their ideas of an ideal existence on the residents.

In 1917, Guamanians who had been nominated by the native residents and approved by the governor assembled in Agana for a congress. These elected officials then met once a month to advise the governor on what was best for the island and its people. Some governors followed the officials' suggestions, but others ignored the congress and imposed their authority over every issue regarding the island.

This seesaw government continued until December 24, 1930, when a democratic-thinking governor wrote a

Citizens of Guam pay tribute to their
island's discoverer, Magellan, in a program
of dances, songs, and speeches performed
by school children. This program took
place in 1932, at which time Guam's bill
of rights was in the process of being approved.

bill of rights for Guam, modeled after the amendments to the U.S. Constitution. This bill of rights did not stay in effect, however. The Department of the Navy did not approve parts of the document, which was revised in 1933 and approved. Although not all governors followed the revised bill of rights exactly, it gave Guamanians some say in their government.

WORLD WAR II

While the United States was establishing itself on Guam, the other Mariana Islands were changing governments. About the time that Governor Leary arrived in Guam, the Germans bought all the islands Spain owned in the Pacific area and colonized some of them. After the Germans lost World War I, the countries that had fought against Germany asked for the colonies.

When the negotiations ended, Japan was made administrator of most of the islands. President Woodrow Wilson protested; he did not want the Japanese to control so much of the Pacific. But he was voted down, and the Japanese began to colonize and fortify the islands. This made Guam, which was only 120 miles (190 km) from the Japanese bases on Saipan, vulnerable to attack.

Japan bombed Guam the same day it bombed Pearl Harbor. When the Guamanians first saw the Japanese planes, they thought they were American planes. But within minutes, bombs started falling on Agana and Apra Harbor, and the islanders knew they were at war. After the bombings, 10,000 Japanese troops landed on several areas around Guam. On December 10, the 350 American sailors and marines stationed on the island tried to defend the government buildings at the Plaza de España in Agana. But the Japanese surrounded them, and Captain George Johnson McMillin gave the order to surrender. Guam was the first U.S. land occupied by enemy forces during World War II.

The Japanese immediately fortified the island with Guamanian labor. The natives lost their homes, they often went hungry, and they prayed for the Americans to return. When American planes and ships attacked the island on June 19, 1944, many Guamanians captured the Japanese soldiers in their villages, and then paddled canoes over reefs to give the Americans information on the Japanese positions.

After more than a month of fighting, the United States regained control of Guam from the Japanese. However, isolated Japanese troops held out until August 10, when the fighting finally ended. A few Japanese soldiers hid in the jungles and were discovered during the next several years. One Japanese sergeant was found twenty-six years after the peace treaty had been signed between the United States and Japan.

REBUILDING GUAM

Guam became the headquarters of the Pacific Naval Forces commanded by Admiral Chester William Nimitz. As commander of the base, he was also governor of Guam. Nimitz found the natives malnourished and living in shacks. Most of them had serious health problems. The situation was bad enough to place a military government on the island, so people could receive help quickly and efficiently.

Military rules were harsh, and civil liberties were suspended, including meetings of the Guam Congress, which was the people's hope for eventual self-government. Public gatherings, with the exception of church services, were not allowed. Residents complained, but the decision to impose the military government helped them return to a better way of life. By May 1946, the military rules gave way to navy rules. Shortly after, the Congress of Guam reconvened and called for the United States to take steps toward the independence of Guam.

Self-government was important, but so was rebuilding. Before the war, Agana was a maze of streets that crisscrossed the city. They were not beautiful, but they were functional. After the rubble of war was cleared, the navy hired a city planner, who laid out wide streets that crossed at well-measured corners. Unfortunately, he did not consider that the land he used to lay out the streets was owned by hundreds of people.

This caused legal problems that are still included in disputes about land-use ownership of the island. Private citizens, the government of Guam, and the U.S. government do not agree on the exact locations and proportions of land used by each, but it is assumed that each controls one-third of the island.

In addition to Agana's streets, a highway was built to connect the newly opened Andersen Air Force Base with the expanded naval bases that now include a submarine base at Apra Harbor. Schools were rebuilt, and the College of Guam opened in 1952. Until then, students who wanted to continue their education had to leave the island.

The building created government jobs for Guamanians. However, the development of private jobs was slow because of the navy's travel restrictions. No one was allowed on Guam without a military security clearance. Planes were allowed to stop and refuel at the naval air base, but passengers could not leave the airport without special permission.

Without free travel to import and export materials, private industries could not develop. This restriction was lifted in 1962, and an international airport was opened northeast of Agana. Now a variety of businesses including ship repairs, furniture building, cement and petroleum products, textile manufacturing, printing, and tourism are on the island.

GOVERNMENT

While industries were growing and living conditions were improving for the people of Guam, Guamanians pursued their goal of self-government. In 1950, responsibility for the governing of Guam passed from the Department of the Navy to the Department of the Interior.

On July 21, 1950, the Organic Act of Guam became law after approval by the U.S. Congress. This document gave Guam a civilian government and made the people U.S. citizens. But even with this new status, they could not elect their governor. Not until 1970 were they permitted to hold an election to choose a governor.

Guam is an unincorporated, organized territory of the United States. It has a nonvoting delegate to the U.S. Congress, and its residents cannot vote in presidential elections. In 1987, Guamanian voters approved a measure asking the U.S. Congress to make Guam an American commonwealth.

EDUCATION

The American bombing of Guam to recapture the island in 1944 damaged or destroyed all the schools except five, which were reopened on October 1, 1944. The U.S. Department of the Navy helped build more schools on Guam and brought teachers from the United States to teach in some of them. Today, most teachers are residents of Guam and teach Chamorro and English, the official languages of the island.

The public school system on Guam is patterned after school systems in the states. Attendance is compulsory for children between the ages of five and sixteen. In addition to the twenty-seven elementary and nine secondary public schools, there are private schools and schools administered by churches. Guam Community College, founded in 1977, has a Micronesian research center and a marine laboratory that attracts students from other Pacific Islands.

SPORTS

Before World War II, baseball was the favorite sport on Guam. On Sundays, families traveled over roads, some no wider than paths, to watch baseball games. It was years after the war ended before Guamanians showed interest in sports again, but today they enjoy playing and watching baseball, football, and basketball. Swimming pools, tennis courts, golf courses, and bowling alleys are found on Guam. Swimming and snorkeling are popular throughout the year, as is cockfighting, which was introduced on the island by the Spanish.

HOLIDAYS AND FIESTAS

One of the most important Guamanian traditions is the fiesta to honor patron saints. Villagers hold a fiesta on the Saturday closest to their patron saint's day. After the Saturday afternoon mass, parishioners carry a statue or relic of their saint throughout the village before they begin their fiesta. Some of the larger villages have floats, and many have games and contests. Every village has music and food. Tables are set up under shelters often made with plaited palm fronds, and the village becomes one big open house. The celebration usually goes on through the night and ends on Sunday evening. The biggest and most important fiesta is held on December 8 to honor Our Lady of the Immaculate Conception, the patron saint of Guam.

Residents also celebrate the same holidays that people celebrate in the states. In addition, Discovery Day is held the first Monday of March to commemorate the day Magellan landed on the island in 1521. Guam Liberation Day on July 21 commemorates Guam's liberation in 1944 from Japanese occupation. And each year on Good Friday, two days before Easter on the Christian calendar, people walk up Mt. Lamlam carrying a cross to commemorate the death of Christ.

TEMPERATURE AND HUMIDITY

Temperatures range from 74° F to 95° F (23° C to 35° C), with an average of 81° F (27° C). Guamanians call their seasons dry and wet. The dry season is from December to May, and the wet season is from June to November, when most of the rain falls. Because humidity is high, especially during the wet season, most houses have heating elements in their closets and cabinets to protect food and personal belongings from mildew. Some people put electric blankets on their beds during the day to keep their sheets dry and their mattresses free of mildew.

FLORA AND FAUNA

Except for cats, dogs, and some farm animals, there are few animals on Guam. *Carabaos*, which are used to do heavy work and to give rides to tourists, are the largest animals on the island.

Guam is free of poisonous snakes and pests. The *Typhlops braminus*, which looks like a large earthworm, is the only common species of snake. A small number of other species were brought in by people or escaped from ships. There are large numbers of iguanas, the most common of which is the yellow-speckled, blackish hilitai, which is about four feet long. There are also small lizards, commonly called *geckos*, that skitter everywhere including in houses, stores, and schools. Because these lizards eat mosquitoes, they are welcomed by residents who must fight the hordes of mosquitoes throughout the island.

Bats are also found on the island. Fruit bats, which feed on fruits, are considered delicacies by some people who eat them on special occasions.

The waters inside the coral reefs are safe for swimming, but sharks and barracudas inhabit the waters outside the reefs. Occasionally, after a typhoon, shark and barracuda notices are posted to warn swimmers that the heavy winds and tides may have forced sharks and barracudas inside the reefs.

The bombing by American planes during the invasion of Guam killed most of the birds on the island. Even today, birds are seldom seen in the capital city of Agana. But several species of birds, including kingfishers and fruit doves, called *tottots*, nest in heavy vegetation throughout the island.

Coconut palms are the most common trees. There are also banana and breadfruit trees and pandamus, called screw pines. The *ifil tree* is the island tree. The island flower is the *bougainvillea* and the island bird is the fruit dove.

SIX

AMERICAN SAMOA

American Samoa is about 2,300 miles (4,325 km) south-west of Honolulu, Hawaii, and is the most southerly land owned by the United States. It has six islands: Tutuila, Aunuu, the three islands of the Manua group: Ofu, Olosega, and Tau, and Rose, an uninhabited coral atoll. Also included as part of American Samoa is Swains Island which is 210 miles (340 km) northwest of Tutuila. The total land area of the islands is 76 square miles (315 sq km). The islands are all peaks of volcanic mountains that rise from the ocean floor. About 34,000 people live on American Samoa, and its capital is Pago Pago.

DISCOVERY AND COLONIZATION

Anthropologists have found evidence that settlers came to the Samoan Islands before 600 B.C. through Indonesia,

AMERICAN SAMOA

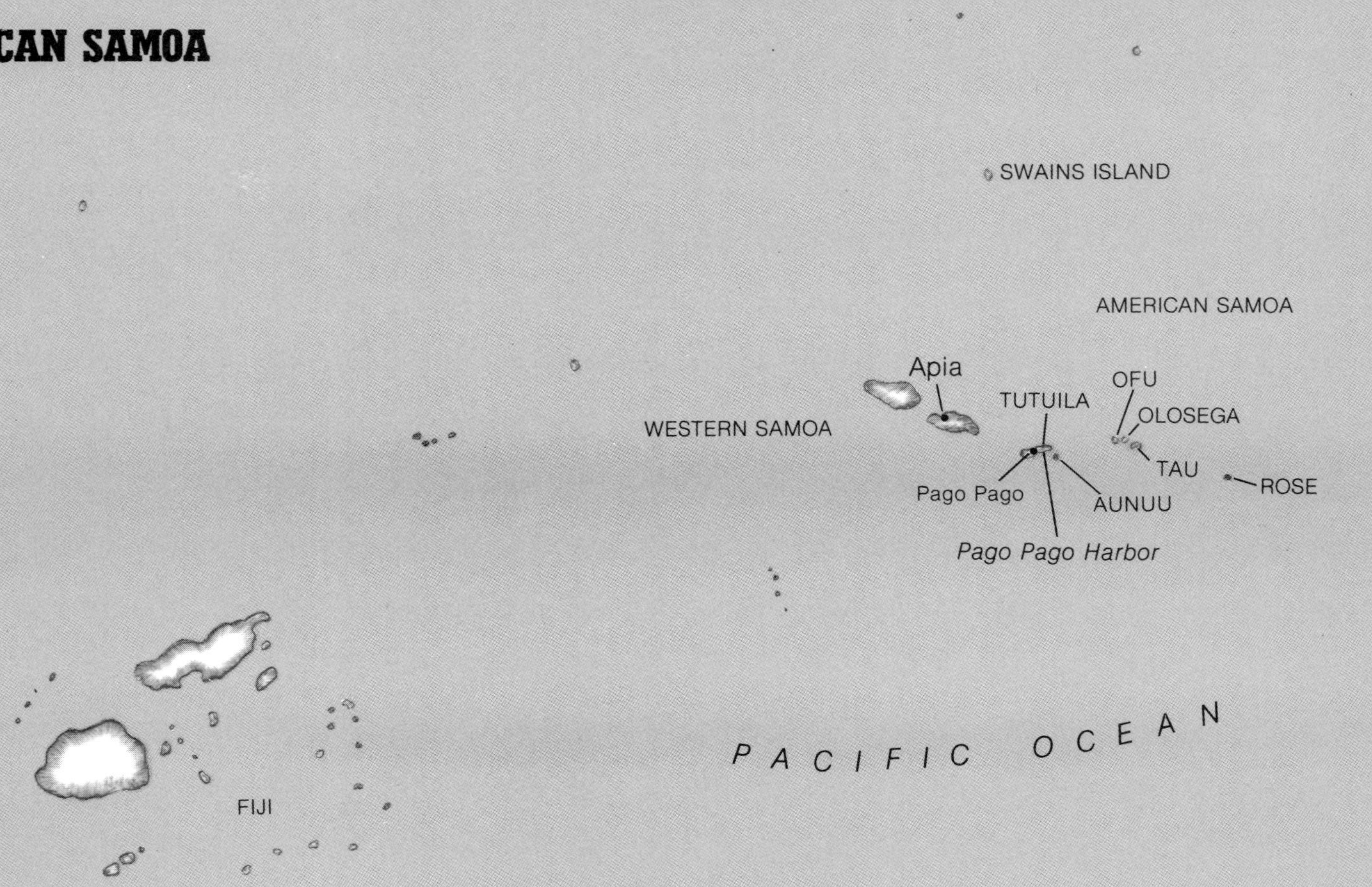

SWAINS ISLAND

AMERICAN SAMOA

OFU
OLOSEGA
TAU
ROSE
AUNUU

TUTUILA

Apia

Pago Pago

Pago Pago Harbor

WESTERN SAMOA

PACIFIC OCEAN

FIJI

the New Hebrides, and Fiji. These natives had contact with people on other South Pacific islands, but were isolated from the rest of the world.

Jacob Roggeveen, a Dutch admiral, saw the islands in 1722 but did not record their position accurately. This gave the natives the opportunity to remain unaffected by other civilizations for another forty-six years. In 1768, French navigator Luis Antoine de Bougainville recorded the correct position of the islands, which helped navigators to find them.

American, British, and French ships often stopped at the islands. In 1824, Otto von Kotzebue, a Russian navigator, docked there. However, the ships were not always welcomed; during one docking natives killed eleven French sailors when they went ashore for fresh water.

But the ships continued to come, and the natives became more friendly. In 1838, the native chiefs agreed to let a British commander use Samoan ports for a fee. The next year Commander Charles Wilkes brought six American ships, which had been outfitted for his scientific expedition of the Pacific. He made maps of the area, while his scientists recorded the local flowers and wildlife.

Wilkes and Chief Malietoa Vainu'upo arranged a treaty with other chiefs that set up rules for visiting ships. Because of Wilkes's help in writing the agreement, he was allowed to raise the American flag on Pago Pago. The chiefs also welcomed British and German traders. Eventually, they allowed men from the United States, Britain, and Germany to settle on the islands and marry native women.

The Americans usually stayed on the eastern islands of Samoa and the British and Germans stayed on the western islands. By the mid-1800s, the chiefs owed British and German traders large sums of money for muskets and ammunition they needed to carry on their fights for territorital rights.

In 1856, August Unshelm arrived in Apia, in what is now Western Samoa. He had developed a colonization plan for Germany in the Pacific, and the annexation of Samoa was part of his plan. Unshelm died in 1861 during a hurricane, but Germany sent Theodor Weber to continue trading and acquiring land. Soon Germany owned 75,000 acres (30,000 ha) in Samoa.

Because ships stopped often at Samoa, whoever controlled the trading, buying, and selling of goods would make a lot of money. To protect these rights from the chiefs and from each other, the United States, Britain, and Germany sent consuls to Apia to discuss the situation. The meeting was not successful. For a time the chiefs were forced to rule under the direction of these consuls and there was dissatisfaction throughout the islands. The chiefs continued to fight among themselves and with the consuls, while the consuls fought with each other and with the chiefs.

Because of these disagreements, Britain sent ships to watch the Germans, and the Americans sent ships to watch the British and the Germans. By 1872, the situation was so tense the chief of Tutuila asked R. W. Meade, commander of the American ship *Narraganset*, to place Tutuila under United States protection. The commander did not have the authority to accept the offer. However, in return for friendship and protection, he signed a treaty with Chief Mauga for the exclusive rights to Pago Pago Harbor. Although this treaty was not ratified by the United States, it accelerated the disagreements among the three nations.

The following year, President Ulysses S. Grant sent Colonel A. B. Steinberger to help the Samoans. Steinberger suggested that the chiefs stop transferring their land to other countries. He also helped with peace negotiations among the chiefs. When he returned to Washington, Steinberger tried to convince the Congress to annex the islands, but Congress refused. Disappointed, Steinberger went back to Samoa to help the people become an independent nation, but the chiefs could not agree on how to reach independence.

With the United States, Britain, and Germany still bickering about their rights, several Samoan chiefs went to Fiji, a British colony, to ask for protection from foreign nations. When the British, who wanted the islands for themselves, would not help them, the chiefs went to Washington, D.C. Although their request for protection was denied, the U.S. secretary of state negotiated the right to use Pago Pago as a coaling and naval station.

In 1879, some chiefs gave Germany almost complete control of the harbor near Apia. During the same year, other chiefs gave Britain the right to build a naval station in the same area. These agreements led to so much tension among these countries that by 1889 warships from all three nations anchored off the islands to protect their citizens.

While the ships were there, a hurricane blew across the area and crashed the German and American ships against the reefs—only the British ship escaped. The loss of several ships and almost 150 people calmed tempers. Instead of fighting, the three countries held a conference in Berlin, Germany. On June 14, 1889, a treaty was signed that declared the Samoan Islands a neutral territory with an independent government to be ruled by a king. The authority of consuls from foreign countries was restricted to Apia and the lands they had bought from the natives over the years.

The islands did not remain independent for long. Continued bickering among the chiefs led to warlike fighting, and in 1899 the consuls annulled the Berlin Treaty. By an agreement signed on December 2, 1899, the Samoan Islands were divided among the three nations. However, Britain gave its land on Samoa to Germany for rights to Tonga and some of the Solomon Islands located in the Pacific.

Under the Berlin Treaty, the United States kept the islands that lie east of longitude 171 degrees, now called American Samoa. Germany took the islands west of the longitude, now called Western Samoa. Germany lost Western Samoa during World War I, when military troops from New Zealand, a British colony, landed on German Samoa. In 1920, the League of Nations gave New Zealand authority to govern Western Samoa.

On November 11, 1946, New Zealand asked the United Nations to place Western Samoa under a United Nations Trusteeship. The Trusteeship became effective on January 25, 1947, and remained until January 1, 1962, when Western Samoa was given independence.

U.S. TERRITORY

The eastern Samoan Islands became American on April 17, 1900, when the flag of the United States was officially

Top: *a cruise ship anchored at Pago Pago Harbor.* Bottom: *a hotel by Pago Pago Bay.*

raised on a hill overlooking Pago Pago Harbor. The chiefs of Tutuila and Aunuu transferred their authority over the islands to the United States on that date, but the chiefs of Manua did not transfer their authority until July 16, 1904. On February 20, 1929, the deeds of transfer were accepted by the U.S. Congress. Swains Island which Britain had given up was annexed by the United States in 1925.

During the forty years before World War II, the Department of the Navy, which was responsible for the new territory and used Pago Pago as a refueling station, paid little attention to the people of American Samoa who were allowed to live under their system of *matais* as they had done for hundreds of years. Matais are the lawmakers born to or elevated to the position.

Under this tradition, each village has one or more extended families called *'aiga*. Each 'aiga chooses a *matai* who sees that land and food are divided fairly. He settles family arguments and sits on the village council which is called a *fono*. The fono sets the rules of the village.

Within the 'aiga there is an unwritten law that people must share what they have with family members and members of their village. Therefore, whatever grows in an 'aiga belongs to the people in that 'aiga. Even fishing rights in lagoons are given to specific 'aigas, and villages must honor those rights.

It was these strict territorital rules that caused fighting among chiefs over the years. The disagreements did not stop entirely after the islands became an American territory. However, with the Americans as negotiators between the feuding families, the problems were usually settled with words instead of ammunition.

The presence of almost 20,000 American troops on

the island during World War II to guard against a Japanese invasion upset village tradition. The Japanese never came, but Americans stayed throughout the war, and many islanders went to work for the military. They developed a liking for American food, clothes, and gadgets. When the war ended in 1945, many workers were left without jobs. They had grown used to having money to buy American goods, and it was difficult to readjust to their old ways of living.

Administration of the islands passed from the Department of the Navy to the Department of the Interior in 1951. Because the budget for the Department of the Interior was small, there was no money for improvements on the islands. Schools and health facilities became inadequate for the growing population. Paint peeled off buildings, foundations rotted, roads filled with ruts, and outhouses overflowed into Pago Pago Bay.

In 1962 when President John F. Kennedy learned of the neglect of the island, he appointed H. Rex Lee as governor and requested action. By the end of the year, Tutuila became an island the United States could be proud to own. Lee stayed for six years and did much to improve the quality of life on American Samoa.

However, these changes may end some of the traditions of the islanders. Many natives today have cars, washing machines, and television sets; they wear American clothes and eat American food they buy in supermarkets. The need for money has created a new way of thinking—the tradition of sharing was one of using instead of owning. People believed that if they did not have something, there was someone who had what they needed and would let them use it. This was called *Fa'a Samoa* which translates to "the Samoan Way." But many people now want to own things and Fa'a Samoa has

become *Fa'a America*, which translates to "the American Way."

INDUSTRY

Almost half of the workers on American Samoa are employed by the government. Commercial fishing fleets and fish canneries also employ a large number of workers. But these are not all American Samoans—many are fishermen from Taiwan, Japan, and Korea. They bring in tuna from areas of the Pacific for the canneries on Tutuila. These employ several thousand Western Samoans who come from their islands to work for minimum wages. American Samoans would be hired, but many of them believe that minimum wage is too little pay for the work.

There is also a factory that manufactures coconut products which, along with the canned tuna, are major exports. Mats, baskets, and other handicrafts are also exported, but this is a small industry. The number of visitors to the islands has been increasing, and some American Samoans own businesses or work for businesses that serve tourists. Still, unemployment is high on the islands, and many people rely on money from the United States for their needs. Because of this and the increasing desire for the American standard of living, thousands are leaving the islands. The departures have been so large that there are now more Samoans living in the United States than there are in American Samoa.

Samoan children playing in the trees of the Samoan jungle

GOVERNMENT

Shortly after the Department of the Interior became responsible for the islands, eight men served as governors during a two-year period. Much of the deterioration on American Samoa after 1951 was caused by the frequent replacement of governors appointed by the President of the United States. These men did not know the needs of the Samoans, and they did not stay long enough to learn. These frequent changes no longer happen.

An agreement that provided for the election of a governor and lieutenant governor, chosen by the people of the islands, was issued on September 13, 1977. On November 8 of that year, the Samoans elected their own governor and lieutenant governor. The islands also have a senate and house of representatives.

American Samoa is an organized, unincorporated territory of the United States. The people are nationals of the United States, not citizens. They have a nonvoting delegate in Congress, but they cannot vote in presidential elections.

Many citizens of American Samoa and Western Samoa hope that the islands will some day be joined the way they once were. This is not an impossible dream, but if the islands do come under one government, it will not be in the near future.

SEVEN

WAKE ISLAND, MIDWAY ISLANDS, AND OTHER SMALL ISLANDS

WAKE ISLAND

Wake Island is in the North Pacific Ocean 2,300 miles (3,685 km) west of Honolulu, Hawaii, and 1,290 miles (2,070 km) northeast of Guam. With Peale Island on Wake's east coast and Wilkes Island on its west coast, the islands form an atoll that has a land area of only 3 square miles (12 sq km). The island group is 5 miles long by 2 miles (8 km × 3 km) wide and forms a V-shape that encloses a lagoon 5 miles long by 3 miles (8 km × 5 km) wide.

The islands had no inhabitants when Captain William Wake, commanding the British schooner *Prince William Henry*, discovered them in 1796. In 1841, Lieutenant Charles Wilkes, a U.S. naval officer on an expedition to explore and survey the Pacific Ocean, gave his name to

WAKE ISLAND, MIDWAY ISLANDS, AND OTHER SMALL ISLANDS

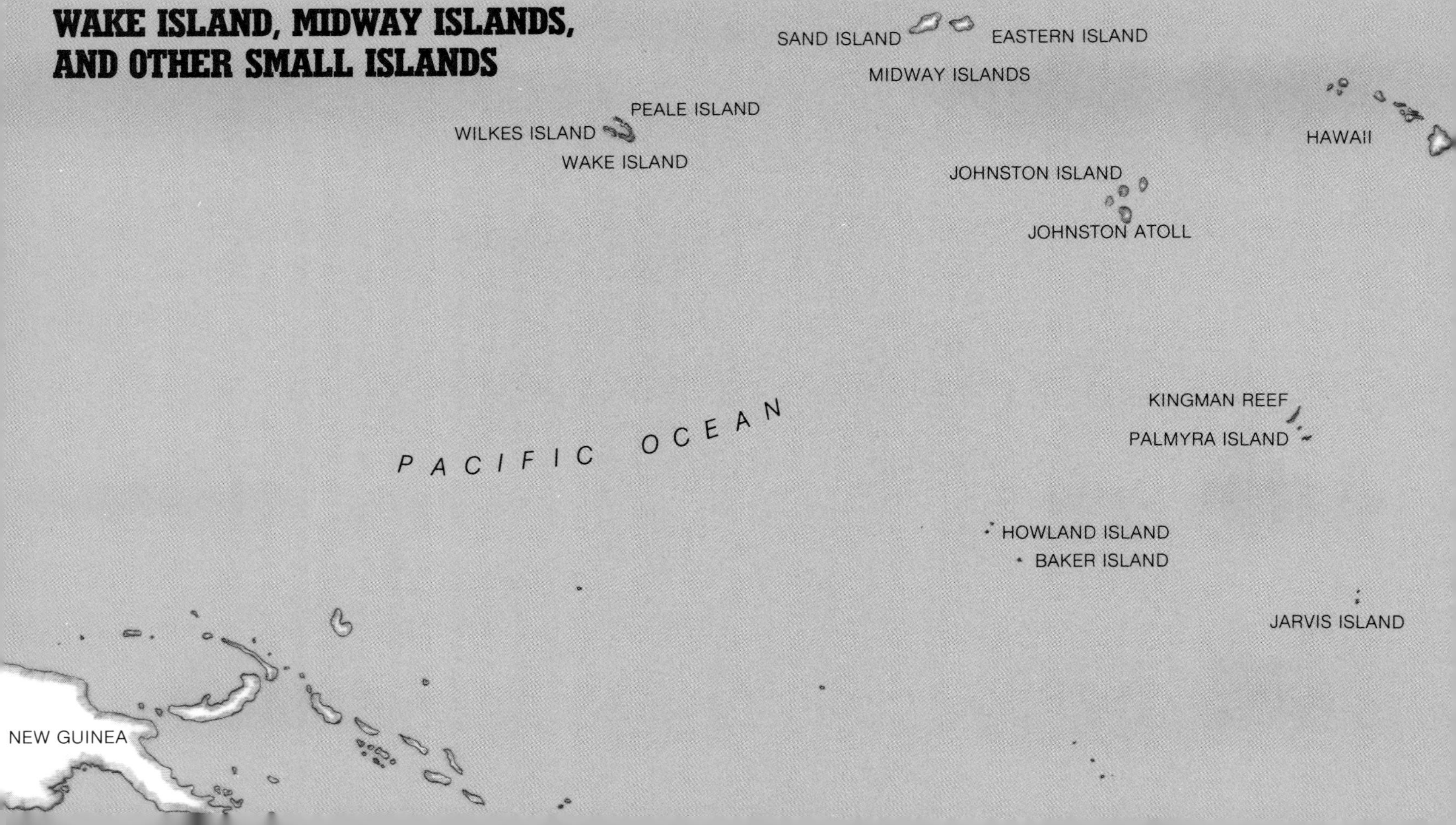

HAWAII

JARVIS ISLAND

KINGMAN REEF

PALMYRA ISLAND

EASTERN ISLAND

SAND ISLAND

MIDWAY ISLANDS

JOHNSTON ISLAND

JOHNSTON ATOLL

HOWLAND ISLAND

BAKER ISLAND

PEALE ISLAND

WILKES ISLAND

WAKE ISLAND

PACIFIC OCEAN

NEW GUINEA

one island. He called the third island Peale to honor Titian Ramsay Peale, an American artist and naturalist who was on the exploring expedition.

Formal possession of the three islands was taken on behalf of the United States by the commander of the *U.S.S. Bennington* on January 17, 1899. The atoll became a naval installation in 1934. The next year, Pan-American Airways built a hotel on Wake Island and used the atoll as a stopover for its flights between the United States and China.

In 1939, the U.S. Congress voted to fortify Wake. More than 1,000 workers were completing construction of an air and submarine base when the Japanese attacked Wake a few hours after they bombed Pearl Harbor on December 7, 1941. Four days later, 400 marines resisted an attack by a Japanese naval task force. The Americans held off the Japanese until December 23, when 1,100 Japanese troops went ashore. Badly outnumbered, the U.S. marines and their commander Major James P. S. Devereux surrendered. On February 14, 1942, a fleet of U.S. ships commanded by Admiral William F. Halsey attacked Wake Island but didn't try to recapture it. The Japanese surrendered on September 4, 1945, to end World War II.

After the war, the U.S. Department of the Navy built living and working facilities and a runway to handle commercial and military planes. The responsibility for Wake Island was transferred from the Department of the Navy to the Department of the Interior by President John F. Kennedy in 1962. Wake is still under that department. However, since June 24, 1972, the local government has been ruled by a code of law written by the Department of the Air Force.

During the Vietnam War, Wake was a stopover for

a state. In 1889, Britain claimed the island. But when the Hawaiian Islands became a territory of the United States, the United States took back complete control of Palmyra.

The United States started building a naval air station in 1938, and the atoll became a landing strip for military planes during World War II. Palmyra is now under the administration of the Department of the Interior and is presently uninhabited.

JOHNSTON ATOLL

Johnston Atoll is in the central Pacific Ocean 700 miles (1,125 km) southwest of Honolulu, Hawaii. Its four islands are Johnston, Sand, Akau, and Hikina. The largest island is Johnston, which has a land area of only 1 square mile (4 sq km).

The atoll had no inhabitants when it was sighted in 1807 by Charles James Johnston, captain of the British warship Cornwallis. Because the atoll was valuable for its guano deposits, which are used for fertilizer, the United States and the Kingdom of Hawaii claimed the atoll in 1858. The dispute of ownership continued while both nations mined the guano deposits. The controversy ended in 1898, when the Hawaiian Islands became a territory of the United States.

The Department of the Navy took over the administration of the atoll on December 29, 1934. In 1941, the island became a naval defense area and Johnston served as a landing strip for military planes during World War II. After the war, the area was used to conduct nuclear tests and store chemical ammunition. Johnston Atoll is administered by the Nuclear Defense Agency under the Department of Defense and has no permanent residents.

KINGMAN REEF

Kingman Reef is in the central Pacific Ocean 920 miles (1,480 km) southwest of Honolulu, Hawaii. The reef is 9 miles (14 km) long by 5 miles (8 km) wide and encloses a lagoon that was used in 1937 and 1938 by seaplanes of Pan-American Airways.

Edmund Fanning, an American naval officer, discovered the reef in 1798. It was named for Captain W. E. Kingman, who rediscovered the reef in 1853. The United States annexed Kingman Reef on May 3, 1922. The reef has been under the jurisdiction of the Department of the Navy since December 29, 1934, and has no permanent inhabitants.

BAKER, HOWLAND, AND JARVIS ISLANDS

Baker, Howland, and Jarvis islands are in the central Pacific Ocean about 1,600 miles (2,575 km) southwest of Honolulu, Hawaii. Howland has a land area of less than 1 square mile (4 sq km). Baker and Jarvis each have 1 square mile (4 sq km) of land.

The islands had no inhabitants when they were discovered in the 1840s. They were claimed by the United States and Great Britain for their guano deposits. From 1850 to 1890, both countries mined the guano. After most of it had been mined, the countries lost interest in the islands.

In 1935, a small group of colonists from Hawaii settled the islands. The following year, the United States Department of the Interior took jurisdiction over the islands. Great Britain did not object.

A landing strip was built on Howland, and it became a refueling stop for planes flying between Hawaii and the

Samoan Islands. In July 1937, Amelia Earhart, the first woman to attempt a flight around the world, left New Guinea for Howland. She and her copilot Fred Noonan never reached the island. What happened to them and their plane is still a mystery. All three islands have been uninhabited since the end of World War II.

NAVASSA ISLAND

Navassa Island is between Jamaica and Haiti in the Caribbean about 100 miles (160 km) south of the U.S. naval base in Guantanamo, Cuba. The island was discovered by Peter Duncan in 1857. The 2-square-mile (8-sq-km) island is uninhabited and has been under U.S. jurisdiction since January 17, 1916. In 1917, the U.S. government built a lighthouse on Navassa and continues to reserve the island for this purpose.

Amelia Earhart poses by her plane.
She was the first woman to cross the
Atlantic Ocean in an airplane. In 1937,
she and her copilot were to arrive on
Howland Island, but never did.

EIGHT

FUTURE OF
THE ISLANDS

In this book, you've traveled from the Caribbean Sea to the central, southern, and western Pacific Ocean and back again. Some of the places you've visited like Navassa, Baker, Howland, Jarvis, and Palmyra islands, Johnston Atoll, and Kingman Reef probably will never have permanent residents. Because of the defense equipment and military installations on Wake and Midway islands, people living there will continue to be military and civilian employees of the U.S. government who live only a year or two on the islands.

Most residents in American Samoa, Guam, the Commonwealth of the Northern Marianas, the Federated States of Micronesia, the Republic of the Marshall Islands, and the Republic of Palau have ancestors who have been on the islands for generations. These ancestors lived simply off the land and the sea. Now many of the younger people are not satisfied with the old ways. They want television sets, tape decks, American-style clothes, and other things they see on television and in movies. But jobs are scarce.

The largest employer on these islands is the U.S. government. The government, however, has jobs for fewer than half of the people. Fishing and agriculture employ a small number of persons. Other industries are few and often include little more than making handicrafts to sell to tourists.

Probably the islands in most need of financial help are the Federated States of Micronesia, the Republic of the Marshall Islands, and the Republic of Palau. They all need schools, roads, more permanent buildings, and industry.

American Samoa has some industry, but it needs more to keep its young people from leaving the island for work. Guam seems to be in a better financial situation than the other Pacific islands; it has a number of small industries and a fairly large tourism business. Because the Commonwealth of the Northern Marianas is near Guam, tourism on the commonwealth is growing and will help residents financially.

Tourism seems to be the ideal industry to develop on islands that have a limited amount of land. But tourism will have to be developed slowly, so the growth won't destroy the culture and beauty that attract tourists.

Puerto Rico and the Virgin Islands have kept their culture and beauty for visitors to enjoy, and tourism has helped the islands financially. Their closeness to the United States has also helped. It does not cost as much to send materials to Puerto Rico and the Virgin Islands as it does to ship things to the Pacific islands. This has made it easier to bring in industries. Also, Puerto Rico and the Virgin Islands are larger than the islands in the Pacific, and they have more space for industry. But Puerto Rico and the Virgin Islands are not without problems.

Puerto Rico has a larger population than its area can support comfortably. It is also almost totally dependent on the United States for its economic growth. Yet, there are many people who do not want more industry. Therefore, although there is room for expansion, industrial development is not growing as fast as it might to support the large number of people. How the island solves its population and economic situation will determine the future standard of living for its residents.

The Virgin Islands have a different kind of problem. There are no permanent streams or underground water supply on the islands, so their industrial development is limited by the lack of water. Desalination plants make it possible for established industries to operate and supply water to the residents and tourists. But until more plants are built, the Virgin Islands are limited in their economic growth and must bring in almost everything they use from the United States.

People and places change. But for years, the one thing that has not changed is the need for financial help from the United States. It appears this need for help will continue, and with it U.S. involvement with these islands throughout the world.

FOR
FURTHER READING

Carpenter, Allen. *Far-Flung America.* Chicago: Children's Press, 1979.

Kahn, E. J. *A Reporter in Micronesia.* New York: W. W. Norton, 1966.

Lerner Publications' Department of Geography. *Puerto Rico in Pictures.* Minneapolis, MN: Lerner Publications, 1987.

Perl, Lila. *Puerto Rico.* New York: William Morrow, 1979.

Rand, Abby. *Puerto Rico and the Virgin Islands.* New York: Scribner's, 1973.

Time-Life eds. *The U.S. Overseas.* New York: Time-Life Books, 1970.

INDEX